The User's Manual

Lumin8 was created after a year of extreme personal loss.

In a single year I lost three of the people closest to me – two of them to cancer.
I created an on-line program to thank and reward those who supported me during this time, and with the exception of the plant spirit portion (which came later), the foundation of Lumin8 was unintentionally created.

The inspiration for Lumin8 came after taking a much-needed healing get-away, where I was formally introduced to plant-spirit medicine.

The information shared in this manual has to do with healing. It also speaks specifically to cancer. You may think, "Well, I don't want to be a healer. I am an intuitive" or "Cancer is NOT my specialty."

Please note: *Manifesting is manifesting.* The stories our body tells constitute "a reading" , cancer related or not.

Please take the information here and apply it across your life (or the lives of those you read). Lumin8 will support any endeavor.

Lumin8 is a practical and magical healing tool for the Urban Shaman. It combines ancient wisdom used for centuries by indigenous cultures—a wisdom lost to "civilized folk."

Lumin8 can be used as an oracle (alone or with a traditional tarot deck). And just as importantly, Lumin8 is a healing tool that supports any modality.

Humans attract everything from health to wealth, dates to mates, or purpose to passion through the energy body.

The objective of Lumin8 is twofold: to mindfully address situations before they are unintentionally manifested in life or the physical body, **and to create** healthy conditions.

The 55-card oracle includes six parts:

- 17 Energy Bodies (including Chakras & Energy Fields)
- 12 Plant Spirits
- 10 Elements
- 6 Bodies of Supporting Entities
- 5 Emotions
- 5 Universal Shapes

Once you understand the theory behind Lumin8, you will come to understand how to use it—for it is a magnificent tool.

Find a brief summary of definitions below, but please note that this intuitive tool has a personal relationship with you, the user.

I offer here a baseline of support, but with this oracle it is my intention that you make it your own—without relying on cookbook definitions, even if they are my own.

Lumin8 Card Key

Image	Key Words
Root Chakra	Family, safety, security
Sacral Chakra	Creativity, intimacy
Solar Plexus Chakra	Power, mental acuity
Heart Chakra	Compassion, connection
Throat Chakra	Truth, communication
Third Eye Chakra	Intuition, visualization
Crown Chakra	Purpose, divine connection
8th Chakra – Portal	Imagination gateway
9th Chakra - Soul Star	Ideals, harmony, soul
10th Chakra - Earth Star	Connection to Earth & Ancestors
11th Chakra - Energy Conversion	Commanding forces
12th Chakra - Field of Human Self	The Divine Human
Dandelion	Detox, inspire
Chamomile	Blood cleanse, and relax
Rose	Love
Lavender	Calming, and pain relief
Mugwort	Strength
Holy Basil	Courage
Nettle	Shields
Calendula	Freeing
Echinacea	Discover the real you
Star of Bethlehem	Hope
Sage	Clears
Rosemary	Protects
Earth	Builds, solidifies, protects
Air	Ideas, thoughts, information
Water	Soothes, heals, cleanses
Fire	Adds excitement, destroys/renews
Star	Purifies and forms
Light	Can produce any desired effect
Wood	Joy, buoyancy, positivity
Metal	Protects and deflects
Stone	Strengthens, holds, toughens
Ether	Holds spiritual truths
Triangle	Vision

Square	Structure
Spiral	Growth
Cross	Relationship
Circle	Individuality
Angels	(Self-explanatory)
Ascended Masters	(Self-explanatory)
Star Beings	Other-worldly beings
Ancestors	(Self-explanatory)
Spirit Guides	(Self-explanatory)
The Creator	(Self-explanatory)
Joy	(Self-explanatory)
Anger	(Self-explanatory)
Fear	(Self-explanatory)
Sadness	(Self-explanatory)
Disgust	(Self-explanatory)
Physical Field	The body
Emotional Field	5 inches from the body
Mental Field	10 inches from the body
Spiritual Field	Arm's length from the body
Soul Self	You - lifetime, after lifetime

To make the best use of this deck, spend time with it. In fact, spend time with one card at a time – particularly the Plant Spirits, Elements and Energy Bodies - so you get an idea of the spirit or energy of the image (where applicable) and create your own personal "Lumin8 Card Key." Regarding the Chakra cards and Energy bodies, spend time finding the healing opportunities in your own fields before exploring others.

"Sit with" five cards a week (Sunday through Thursday). You may think "sit with" is a pretty broad guidance, but there are many intuitive types. Your intuitive strengths may be very different than someone else's. (To understand how your intuition speaks to you, take the Intuitive Type Test here: http://ginaspriggs.guru/free-stuff/

Your Intuitive Type is based on your energetic gift order. (Be sure to go take that test!)

Which Type are you? Here is a list of the six basic Intuitive Types:

1. Physical Intuitives sense things with their body. So, sit with a card and see what you feel with it, and from there, what comes to mind?(13)

2. Emotional Intuitives sense information emotionally. If this is you, what emotions and memories come up for you when sitting with a card? (14)

3. Visual Intuitives sense information visually, with their inner eye. If this sounds like you, you will first get movies or pictures in your mind's eye—messages to tell you how the spirit of this image supports you.

4. Auditory Intuitives hear information and guidance. If this is you, then songs, phrases and/or words may pop up. Take note.

5. Mental Intuitives sense by knowing. Information arrives. It often comes on demand and it requires a lot of trust. (12)

6. Spiritual Intuitives sense the invisible energies surrounding them. If this is you, allow the guidance that comes with the presence of the Angels, Ascended Masters, Spirit Guides, Star Beings and the Creator.

Many people have a few of these heightened senses—while some people have them all! The best way to get to know your Lumin8 Oracle is to connect with the cards intuitively.

The Exercise: Date with Lumin8! Your "Journey Work"

Journeying is a process used by many indigenous cultures to gain insight and information. Many require the use of drumming to support attainment of the "alpha state." I can personally journey at a moment's notice. In the journeying process, we must all honor our wisdom and needs.

Start by "grounding." This means calling all of our energy into the body, and connecting with the Earth. (If you need support, I share a great Total Healing Meditation, which supports grounding at http://ginaspriggs.guru/free-stuff/)

Start with the card of your choice at the time of your choice, and follow these steps:

- After grounding in a quiet space where you will be undisturbed (yes, that means turn off your phone), get a sense of how you are feeling physically, emotionally, mentally and spiritually. I call this "taking inventory." It provides the baseline you need to discern between intuitive information and "you."

- Pull your selected card and stare at it.

- Now breathe in this image on the card as you continue to stare at it.

- Close your eyes and keep picturing the image on the card.

- Imagine the card as a "window you climb into." From this position you interact with the Plant Spirit, Emotion, Shape, Entity or Element to create your Personal Lumin8 Key. You may find that some of your key words match mine. You may also find that some of them are opposite. Mostly, you will discover more to add. There is no right or wrong.

Using the template on the following pages, make your personal Lumin8 Key Chart.

And in the second half of this book, you'll find ample space for journaling. Use the space to record your personal insights.

Personal Lumin8 Key

Image	Key Words
Root Chakra	
Sacral Chakra	
Solar Plexus Chakra	
Heart Chakra	
Throat Chakra	
Third Eye Chakra	
Crown Chakra	
8th Chakra – Portal	
9th Chakra - Soul Star	
10th Chakra - Earth Star	
11th Chakra - Energy Conversion	
12th Chakra - Field of Human Self	
Dandelion	
Chamomile	
Rose	
Lavender	
Mugwort	
Holy basil	
Nettle	
Calendula	
Echinacea	
Star of Bethlehem	
Sage	
Rosemary	
Earth	
Air	
Water	
Fire	
Star	
Light	
Wood	
Metal	
Stone	
Ether	
Triangle – Vision	
Square – Structure	
Spiral – Growth	

Cross – Relationship	
Circle – Individuality Angels	
Ascended Masters	
Star Beings	
Ancestors	
Spirit Guides	
The Creator	
Joy	
Anger	
Fear	
Sadness	
Disgust	
Physical Field	
Emotional Field	
Mental Field	
Spiritual Field	
Soul Self	

Personal Notes:

Using Lumin8: The Points of Difference

When you sit with a few of the cards, you begin to understand how Lumin8 is unique. The Lumin8 Healing Oracle can be used in a variety of ways:

- To provide Intuitive Readings
- To support Energy Work
- To support Journey Work (*which you may have done by now*)
- To create Sacred Space
- Each portion of the deck can be used separately for divination.

Intuitive Readings: Lumin8 can be used in parts, or as a complete deck - as an oracle. It can also partner with your traditional tarot or other oracles.

Divining with Shapes: This portion of the deck is inspired by *"The Preferential Shape Test"* created by Angeles Arrien. The 5 Universal Shapes are external symbols of internal/psychic states.

Your Self-Reading: The best way to start with shapes? Using your own experience. By using yourself as a "guinea pig" you will see just how much information is revealed through five simple shapes.

Extract Lumin8's 5 shape cards. Lay them out before you (or your client) in order of preference.

Position 1: This position represents where you think you are, because it is where your focus is. It reveals your current source of inspiration or current idea of the future.

△ vision

Position 2: This position represents your motivation. It indicates areas of your nature where you are fluent, strong and resourceful. It reveals your talents, gifts and skills that support the growth you are experiencing in position 3.

☐ structure

Position 3: The shape you place here reveals your true current-growth process. This is where you are at your core. Placing the shapes is an unconscious process, but you are practicing awareness—which allows you to manifest your fullest potential at this time.

◎ Growth

Position 4: This position represents your motivation, which reflects past challenges and circumstances that have inspired your current process of change.

 ✚ relationship

Position 5: This position represents old or unfinished business. It may be a process you dislike, have outgrown, or resist. You will reclaim or revisit it at a later time.

oindividuality

Deeper Meanings of the 5 Shapes

The Circle: This symbol represents wholeness, independence and individuation; development of personal identity; the need for the space to allow this to come to being.

The Equidistant Cross: This symbol represents relationship, integration, balancing and/or coupling, as well as the connection between heaven and earth and human. The need is for healthy connection, whether with a person, project, group or one's self.

The Spiral: This symbol represents the process of growth and evolution. Here, we revisit the same opportunity repeatedly with the renewed perspective that comes from experience.

The Triangle: This symbol represents visions, dreams and objectives that come from revelations, self-discovery and attainment.

The Square: This symbol represents stability, structure, foundations and security. The attraction of this shape indicates that you are ready to initiate a plan.

Divining the Energy Bodies

Lumin8 – a healing tool – supports the petitioning of energies and forces that support the healing process.

The Lumin8 Oracle includes 12 chakras and 5 energy bodies. The possibilities in using this aspect of the deck as an oracle are endless, but I offer here a simple yet effective technique. *Knowledge of the chakras supports this technique. (For advanced learning on chakras, look into taking the Lumin8 On-Line Program.)

Step 1. Extract the 7 in-body chakra cards. *Most people are versed in the 7 in-body chakras but not the 5 out-of-body chakras. This is a good base-line.

Step 2. Shuffle, then layout the cards in a straight line. Note which cards are reversed and elevate them, so that they are higher than the cards that are upright.

Step 3. Review the cards that are reversed. What chakras/areas of life contain the strongest healing opportunities? **Example:** *I extract the first through seventh chakra cards and notice that the first chakra is reversed. Using the chart on page 17, I see that the person I am reading may have issues with her hips. She may also have financial concerns or challenges getting pregnant.*

Step 4. Now extract and shuffle the energy body cards.

Step 5. Place the energy body cards over the reversed chakra cards to determine which energy body contains the healing opportunity. *Whether reversed or upright, the energy body cards let you know what field contains the healing opportunity. There are 5 field cards. In the event that the healing opportunities are more than 5, **address the initial 5 first. Example**: Laying the energy body cards, I see that synchronicity allowed the mental body card to rest on the first chakra card. This tells me that the healing opportunities are around beliefs. I can now ask my client what beliefs she has that are holding this energy in place.*

Step 6. Extract the Emotion cards to determine which emotions are stuck in which field. Often, the stuck emotions originated at the time the compromised chakra was in development. **Example:** *After determining the chakra and energy body – I now find the emotion stuck in that area in sadness. In questioning my client I discover that as a child she wasn't able to get a toy she really wanted because her parents didn't have the money. Now, having money comes with guilt because she is doing better than her parents, financially.*

Step 7: (Bonus Step for Healers): Determine the Supporting Entities, Elements, and/or Plant Spirit Medicine(s) available to support the healing, by taking the remaining cards, shuffling them and extracting one for each compromised chakra. **Example: Air, Star, and Rose.** *First, we use the element of Air to eliminate the beliefs that support the guilt. Then we call in Star Spirit Energy to bring in Spiritual Truths around abundance. Finally, we suggest that the client drink rose petal tea or use rose oil—for gentle love, encouragement and support. The next visit should be scheduled within 2 - 4 weeks to determine progress and energy shifts.*

Creating Sacred Space

Wherever you spend the most time should be sacred for you. And if you are a professional healer, that space is not only sacred for you but for your clients too.

To create sacred space, invite the energies from each direction (East, West, North, South, Above, Below, and Within. (For me the relationship looks like this: Earth/East; Air/North; Water/West; Fire/South; Star/Above; Wood/Below; Within/Heart Chakra) *In my personal practice I often create an altar using a white candle and 1 - 4 cards related to the additional energies I'll request support from.

You can access the healing energies of Plant Spirit and the Elements to create the perfect Sacred Healing Space for you and your client.

Step 1. Determine what energies can support the space or healing process. Extract those cards.

Step 2. Petition or call in the energies you want present – in your personal space and in sessions with your client.

Step 3. Place the Lumin8 Cards next to a lit, white candle.

Step 4. *For an Energy Healing Session, perform the session with attention focused toward staying open to intuitive insight and information.

Step 5: After the session, and before the client leaves, face and thank each of the directions/energies to close the space. *(This can be done silently, but must be done.)*

Energy Sessions

If you are already a Healer or have studied at least one healing modality, Lumin8 will further support your healing sessions.

In a healing session there are energies at work that support us and our clients. These unseen energies guide us to insight, information and practical applications of the information received from within. Opportunity to receive depends on our *remaining open to receiving* – and *trusting* the information received.

Lumin8 contains 38 energies we can petition for healing:

- 12 Plant Spirits
- 10 Elements
- 6 Bodies of Supporting Entities
- 5 Emotions
- 5 Universal Shapes

The opportunity in this section is to understand what we do and why.

With many of the modalities I have learned, the biggest challenge resulted from the fact that the teachers explained what to do but did not explain why. I found this frustrating. Apparently, many teachers do not know why they do what they do – they're just following the directions they were given.

My intention here is to be sure you have a full understanding of why, so you can layer and cross-pollinate what you already know with the Lumin8 Healing Oracle. For this reason, we will go very deep with the healing portion. You will notice that I lean towards the energy of cancer. My healing journey with cancer, and the people I lost to cancer are the reason why I direct much of the teaching around cancer. Please note: I mentioned earlier, manifesting is manifesting. Whether you are treating cancer or the common cold, there are either spiritual, mental, emotional or physical components to be addressed – often all four.

*I also offer an online program and live program – so you can go as deep as you are ready to go.

Are you ready?

Where science sees disease, the alternative practitioner looks for imbalances that need correction… imbalances as individual as the person experiencing the symptoms.

Where the medical community notes pain and offers medication, the alternative care provider seeks to access reasons for the problem, while empowering the client with tools and practices that leave no side effects.

Where traditional medicine refers to the odds, healers look at the individual.

Welcome to the World of Alternative Healing

All living things are formed by fields that can be measured. The best time to create change is before the physical appears from energetic influences – in other words, before energy manifests into matter.

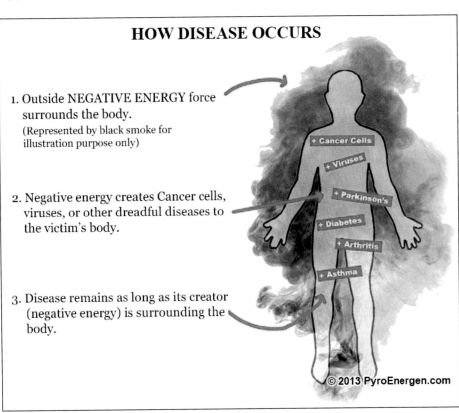

HOW DISEASE OCCURS

1. Outside NEGATIVE ENERGY force surrounds the body. (Represented by black smoke for illustration purpose only)

2. Negative energy creates Cancer cells, viruses, or other dreadful diseases to the victim's body.

3. Disease remains as long as its creator (negative energy) is surrounding the body.

+ Cancer Cells
+ Viruses
+ Parkinson's
+ Diabetes
+ Arthritis
+ Asthma

© 2013 PyroEnergen.com

When it comes to healing (or manifesting), many approaches work some of the time but none can be trusted to work all of the time with all people. We are all individuals with individual causes for illnesses.

One person's cancer may be caused by an energy collection of repressed feelings, with a dash of environmental exposure. Another person's cancer can be triggered by anger, timing, and epigenetics.

One of the biggest frustrations I have with some healers is how they tell the clients they somehow brought an illness on and somehow deserve it. (This may be my reaction because I felt so much shame when I was diagnosed with cancer).

Know this: Illness is no one's "fault." No one deserves to feel sick.

"Congratulations! You have cancer!"

The above words may appear insensitive, but that's exactly what I am inclined to say when someone tells me of that diagnosis.

All illnesses (including cancer) as well as all life challenges invite us to experience a journey that brings us to the places of ourselves and to areas of our lives that need love and attention.

As we set out to heal our self, we uncover the needs, powers and abilities that make us a Light Being on our Divine Mission.

In the end, illness becomes our reason for realizing our personal Divinity.

All illnesses are a call to wholeness.

So you call yourself a Healer?

On page 10 in *The Intuitive Adviser,* the author (Dr. Mona Lisa Schultz) insinuates that "true healers" have experienced at least one major surgery or life-threatening disease. Nothing can be further from the truth. Being a Healer is not predicated on serious health challenges.

The truth is that we all have healing abilities. When we hug someone when they're sad, we are healing them. When you kiss your child's boo-boo to make the pain go away, you are a Healer. When you listen to a friend who is sad, angry, in pain or frustrated, you are a Healer.

Ever see a husband who eats for two just like his pregnant wife? He's a Healer too.

Have you ever cried over the news? Guess what??? HEALER!

The compassion you feel as a Healer allows you to care enough to take action in a big way.

Foundation

Everything (I mean everything) in the universe is made of energy. Energy is a combination of two forces: information and vibration.

So, for example, the cells in your hair vibrate at a different speed than the cells in your brain. Also, energy/information makes "a couch" a couch. Contrasting frequencies are one of the indicators of difference between hair, brain and couch. Energy also contains information that instructs movement and purpose.

In *The Heart's Code*, by Dr. Paul Pearsall, we find that "energy is full of information that instructs it what to do. Vibration plus information (informed vibration) makes everything in the world."

So energy by itself is neither "good" nor "bad." Some energies create a table. Some energies create a dog. If the table has a loose leg and it falls over, it can be considered "bad."

Or the dog can bark all night and be considered bad. But energy is energy. *It's what the thing is doing that makes it "good" or "bad."*

When we look at health we want to determine the energies that are helpful and the energies that are harmful.

Simply thinking something is "good" or "bad" does not make it so. Reality is based on a limited level of specific awareness.

4 Levels of Awareness

As a teacher and healer, I work with the 4 Levels of Awareness. The levels of awareness I am introducing here are based on the four directions. Each direction represents a different kind of energy. In the Lumin8 Oracle, each direction is represented by a specific element.

I am a trained Master Tarologist. And in tarot, each suit represents a certain direction and certain energy.

- The energy of the East represents the suit of pentacles and has to do with things of a **physical** nature.
- The energy of the West represents water, and has to do with things of **emotional** nature.
- The energy of the North has to do with air and represents things **mental** in nature.
- The energy of the South represents the element of fire and has to do with things of a **spiritual** nature.

Different cultures have different ways of viewing the 4 directions but the meanings remain the same: energies are physical, emotional, mental, and spiritual.

You may not call yourself a Shaman or even be interested in tarot, but do understand that these truths have been common knowledge to indigenous cultures for centuries. My direction/element association may be quite different than what you have learned. Go with what makes sense to you.

These four levels of awareness have also been appreciated in major spiritual disciplines, including Judaism, Christianity, Islam, and Buddhism.

Ancient civilizations (including Egyptian, Mayan, Native American, Hindu, and Chinese) were schooled on energy organs.

You may know them as **chakras**.

Chakras are energy organs and as real as your physical organs, but they are invisible. Studies are now validating the existence of chakras. In 1994, Dr. Valerie Hunt performed a study that actually created audiotapes of *chakra sounds.*

Just as your liver transmutes blood and your pancreas alters hormones, chakras serve a certain purpose. **They transform energy from one form to another.**

Chakras vibrate at speeds invisible to the naked eye. Their speeds of vibration are at an etheric level and their sounds of a higher octave than we can perceive.

Disease, illness, and undesirable situations are based on energy. To remedy any disease or change any unwanted situation, we must change the basics of the energy causing it.

Lumin8 will teach you to Stretch your Mind

We're not speaking here of the brain, but of the mind.

The mind is the energetic aspect of self, and with our permission it can access information traveling faster than the speed of light.

We're speaking now of using our intuition. My Mastery Students experience just how powerfully accurate information via our intuition is. They have learned to apply that information in their personal and professional lives.

Intuition uses information already within us. The best tools we have are your imagination and our intent.

In order to make the best use of the information in this Lumin8 Manual, you will need to understand two things: chakra basics, and your intuitive type.

The next page features a **Basic Chakra Chart.** Get to know this chart. It will support your work as a healer and intuitive.

Chakra	Color	Location	Physical	Emotional	Beliefs about (Mental)	Spritual
1st	Red	Womb/Hips	Genitals/Adrenals	Primal feelings	Safety & Security	Deserving to exist
2nd	Orange	Abdoman	Intestines, overies; teste	All feelings	Creative Self Expression	Expressing feelings
3rd	Yellow	Solar plexus	Digestive organs	Fear & self esteem	Power & Success	Empowerment
4th	Green	Heart	Heart, breast, lungs	Emotions in relationship	Love	Connection to God
5th	Blue	Throat	Auditory, mouth, thyroid	Expressions of emotions	Communication	Getting Guidnace
6th	Purple	Forehead	Eyes, Pituitary	Self acceptance	Self Image	Vision & Futuring
7th	White	Top of head	Higher learning/Purpose	Spiritual Nature	Spiritual purpose	Spirituality
8th	Black	1" above head	Thymus	Feelings from past even	Power & use of power	Shamanic abilities
9th	Gold	Arm length up	Diaphragm	Feelings w/in our soul	Idealism	Unity, Harmony
10th	Brown	1 foot under	Feet, bones	Ancestral beliefs	Nature & Ancestors	Spirit in nature
11th	Pink	Around body	Connective Tissue	Forceful feelings	Right to lead & Command	Commanding
12th	Clear	outside 11th	32 points around the bod	Feelings about being tru self	Personal Talents, Gifts, skil	Mastery

Using your intuition and the chart above, determine what chakra houses which illness.

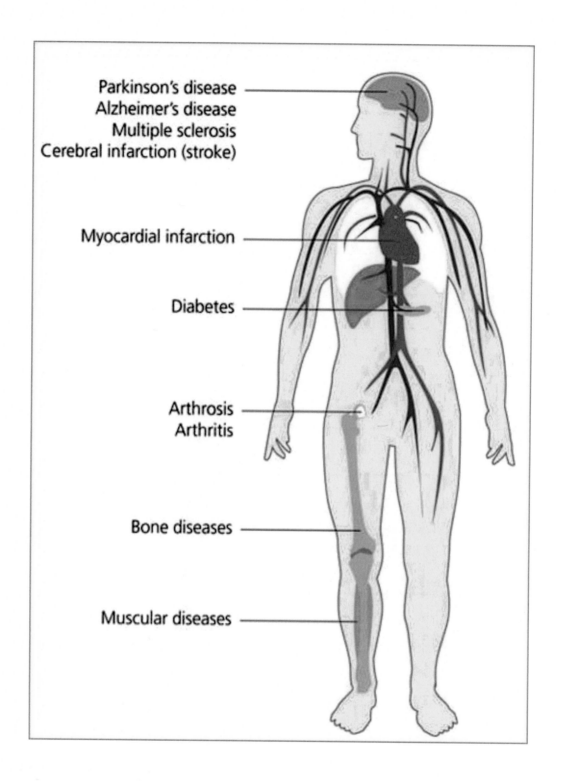

Parkinson's disease
Alzheimer's disease
Multiple sclerosis
Cerebral infarction (stroke)

Myocardial infarction

Diabetes

Arthrosis
Arthritis

Bone diseases

Muscular diseases

What illness is governed by which chakra(s)?
Name the emotional, mental & spiritual components that may be involved.

(4 Levels of Awareness Continued…)

The first steps in any type of healing: (1) **study the situation**, including trying to pinpoint the cause of the condition; (2) **arrive at a strategy**.
Shamans would call this "tracking".

Any **mental beliefs or emotional components that supported the illness** should be evaluated. Cancer, for example, is often created through an emotional contagion. (Doctors are not talking about this yet…but YES, you can "catch cancer.")

In addition there are **physical** ways that cancer can be caught, beyond being exposed to an area leaking radiation.

The **Cancer/Spiritual** connection is huge. It includes (but is not limited to) your own life purpose.

Cancer and all diseases result from cells going out of tune with the rest of the body and ultimately with the spiritual self.

If we want to change the reality of illness, we have to change the physical, emotional, mental and or spiritual reality that created it.

> Truth: Medicine is blind to health.

There are two main types of energy:

Tachyons: Energy faster than the speed of light – also known as intuitive energy.

Quarks: Sensory energy, such as sounds and what we can physically see and touch.

Illness is held within three energy types:

Electrons, which hold a negative charge.
Protons, which hold a positive charge.
Neutrons, which hold a neutral charge.

All illnesses boil down to an off or imbalanced charge, or harmful information held within a charged particle.

Diagnosing the charge of an illness is a useful tool in determining the healing technique.

You will learn here some ways of evaluating a chakra, and use intuition to sense colors, symbols, sounds, numbers and other information within the chakra and the auric field. You will easily see how Lumin8 supports a healing journey.

Energy Tracking & 4-Way Healing

We perform Intuitive Diagnoses through a process called "Energy Tracking." Tracking allows us to zero in on the area of concern so we can determine the basis of the "original wound" or "root cause."

Fear is often a major contributing factor. The core fear is strongest in the part of the body, aspect of the self, the chakra, and the pathway that holds the cause for the illness. Find the fear, and you uncover the root of the illness.

With **4-Way Healing**, your whole self embraces your fearful self and provides the comfort and reassurance you need to conduct the healing process.

> Truth: Often, the cure is the cause.

In reviewing the above, you already have some clues to energy tracking.

1. Note the part of the body of the original site of the illness.
2. Give attention to the varying aspects of the self: physical, emotional, mental and spiritual.
3. Note the chakra related to the original site.
4. Note the energy field of the energy center to be addressed.

From here, we will determine the pathway in alignment with your spirit.

> The 7 Major Lies:
> 1. Evil   4. Power
> 2. Death   5. Suffering
> 3. Judgement   6. False miracles
>   7. Endings
> *More is shared on the 7 Major Lies in The On-Line Program

The Primary Way: The Primary Way has its name not because it is the best but because it is the most commonly used. It combines allopathic and alternative treatments. It uses essential oils, crystals, sound, symbols, colors, numbers, and shapes. It deals with feelings, emotions, and beliefs, as well as nutrition and exercise. It works with energetic layers of the auric field. It attains a neutral state via the chakras and other energy bodies.

The Influential Way: This healing path borrows the influence of spiritual energetic forces and directs their healing energies through the chakra "seal" (*concave bowl at the center of each chakra). We focus on the illness and clarify its cause, surround an unhealthy cell with loving, healing energy, or (my personal favorite) energetically "move aside" and let the entities do their work. This path can also enhance standard treatment and support your body in achieving a balanced state.

The Visionary Way: This process involves shifting energies from other time spaces and dimensions through the center of a chakra, and the use of symbols to hold new energies. Ultimately the goal here is to achieve a neutral space within a chakra center so the healing options are created, and then healing decisions made. Using quantum-creative magic you can either boost current methods of slow treatment or support your body with immediate shifts towards heath.

The Sacred Way:
Here, you activate a quality of truth that combats one of the *7 major lies* and accept grace.

4-Way Healing requires both confidence and caution. These practices are safe, and it is suggested that you use them in combination with your own research on traditional protocols, based on your specific needs. *For example, a tumor is in fact a protective casing around a harmful energy. Traditional protocols require biopsies; however, biopsies can spread the cancer-causing energy, particularly if it is in combination with numerous lymph node removals after surgery.*

4-Way Healing techniques combined with The Lumin8 Healing Oracle can significantly boost the effectiveness of traditional and other alternative treatments. Remember, all disease boils down to a problem with information and vibration.

Solve a problem at the **Primary** level and you solve the problem. Working at this level, we're working with the physical matter of which we are all made.

All spirituality emphasizes the types of powers and forces available through the **Influential** path. Prophets, masters, gurus and common people (like me and you) have access to forces, elements, angels, ascended masters, and ancestors to perform healing work on the self and others.

The magic of the **Visionary** way is basic Shamanism, a form of healing that cuts across all time periods and cultures. Quantum science is emerging with more and more proof of existence of other worlds. Stephen Hawking insists that we exist in at least 11 different dimensions. Shamans have been working through these dimensions, performing "magic for others," since the beginning of time.

Finally, on the **Sacred** path, we are petitioning to the All that is, which is greater than ourselves. Prayer, faith and belief are now techniques validated by science. Doctors often suggest them as a "last resort"—when in fact they should be our first resort. When we petition to the Great Spirit, we're also aligning to the Divine part of ourselves.

Through **4-Way Healing**, we are invited to find the real cause for our illness in order to be restored to wholeness. We must learn to look, listen, feel, and speak through our hearts.

Cross-section of a Chakra

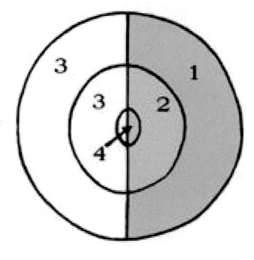

Back of the Chakra (the antii-world)

Front and Center of the Chakra

1. Outer wheel
2. Inner wheel
3. Imagination lens/mirror
4. Center/alchemical spark

Chakras & Cancer: A chakra may store *cancer-creating energies* "in" or "on" the organ it is linked to.

This chart is a "cheat sheet" to support your tracking process.

1st Chakra	2nd Chakra	3rd Chakra	4th Chakra	5th Chakra	6th Chakra	7th Chakra
Adrenal	Colon	Stomach	Heart	Thyroid	Pituitary	Pineal
Cervical	Prostate*	Liver	Breast	Larynx	Eye (L)	Hypothalamus
Vaginal	Ovarian	Pancreas	Lung	Oral		Brain
Skin*	Uterine	Gall Bladder	Esophageal	Lymphatic		Immune system Cancer
Rectal	Kidney*	Spleen		Tracheal		
Prostate*	Bladder	Adrenal		Hodgkin's Disease		
Testicular*		Kidney		Non-Hodgkin's lymphoma		

TIP: Start your work at the lowest compromised chakra or primary site.

After the Logical Process:
Once you have moved through the logical process, use your intuition to gain more insight and clarity.
Use any or all of the following intuitive tools:

- If you are visual, access your inner eye.

- If you are kinesthetic, feel into your body for physical and emotional information.

- If you are auditory, do you get messages or tones? There are many theories on what tone applies to which chakra.

- Also, open yourself to Divine knowing.

Tips on Working with Chakras

When working with your clients or yourself, these tips can support your process:

- Apply your intuition to see, feel and hear the chakras and energy fields in your mind's eye.
- If you choose to use a pendulum, know that you are generally measuring the outer wheels.
- The **left side** of your body (and chakras) processes information considered feminine – feelings, the unconscious, issues about receiving, and spirituality.
- The **right side** of your body (and chakras) deal with the masculine energies—those concerning everyday life and accomplishments, and issues about giving, conquering, and action.
- Because chakras have an inner and outer wheel, **both should be spinning in rhythm with each other**. If they are not, there could be an issue in the field that has (or has not) yet reached the physical body.
- **The inner wheel** regulates the unconscious energy controlled by that chakra and can connect you to various planes and zones of existence, other worlds, and other dimensions.
- **The outer wheel** is your energetic contract between the above realities and the external world. It is primarily affected by your here-and-now conscious life thoughts.

*Generally, both wheels move clockwise, pulling necessary energy from various planes and worlds to enable a healthy life. Reverse or counterclockwise spins sometimes indicate a release of toxins. For example, during a woman's menses, her chakras will spin backwards.

Note: For those 85% of us whose chakras spin clockwise, *a continual reverse spin* (anywhere but in the inner wheel of the 8th chakra) indicates disease and a loss of necessary life energy.

The chakra affecting and affected by illness will be in an abnormal shape. (A healthy chakra is circular.)

- Various geometric shapes can affect energy. You can intuitively spy chakras to see if there are any shapes or forms involved. You can diagnose the problems on various cancers by observing a chakra's shape and sometimes "hold the healing" using other or corrected shapes.
- Generally the lower the chakra, the more slowly it should be moving. When wheels within a certain chakra form moving contrary speeds with each other, or are out of rhythm with the other chakras, you should evaluate for bad programming or disease.

Encoded in each chakra are symbols and numbers holding that chakra in alignment with our spiritual programming. By evaluating numbers and symbols you can determine the injury to the chakra or any other integral elements of illness. You can also "heal" using symbols.

Your Auric Field

Your **chakras** run the inside of you, while your **auric field** regulates the outside of you. There are twelve basic bands in your auric field, just as there are twelve chakras. The two sets of energy organs are paired. The 1st chakra for instance, is partnered with the 1st band of the auric field, and so on. Because of this partnership, changes you make through your chakras are automatically translated into your auric field, and vice versa. The purpose of the auric field is to create boundaries that protect you by screening information. Information has to pass through the perimeters of your field to make it to your chakras (and therefore your body).

Your aura also acts as a screen. Information sent from your chakras pass through the screen of your aura to be delivered into the world. Information from the world also has to pass through the screen to get to your chakras.

Regarding illness, it is very important to establish the correct relationship between these two energy bodies. You might really want to heal from cancer while carrying a program in your auric field that neglects to communicate this desire to the world. This will make it hard to attract the kinds of healers and support needed to gain optimum assistance. The purpose of undergoing chemotherapy is that it wipes out cancer. Unless your auric field breathes, passing out the toxins, the poisonous aftereffects of the chemotherapy can remain in your body and potentially create a new and different cancer.

Hot Tip: In my work I have noticed that we receive *(catch)* intuitive (fast moving) information through certain energy centers, and communicate *(throw)* fast moving information to the world via other energy centers. I refer to this as "catching and throwing." We may be energetically predisposed to receive illnesses through the same energy centers where we are intuitively strong.

Your Energy Egg

The energy egg is an electromagnetic body that penetrates and surrounds the 12 chakras and auric bands. It creates the outer rim of the human energy system, psychically appearing as a pulsating 3-layer field of incandescent energies. Working with the energy egg for healing helps achieve several goals:

- We can clear programs or beliefs in the subconscious and conscious that may be causing illness and problems.
- We can connect our higher consciousness to our everyday world so we can track our highest desires.
- We can diagnose and then release negative information and energies causing the illness.
- We can attract spiritual energies or waves that create real and permanent changes in health and happiness.

To work with your energy egg you must understand it's structure and how it works with your chakras and auric fields in relationship with your programming.

Energy Egg Structure

There are three layers to energy egg. You can connect to any of the layers at will through your pineal gland. (You will most likely link only with the innermost layer until you have achieved a relatively high state of consciousness.)

- **This first layer** is of the energy egg relays information/energy between your body, and inner psyche, and the world.
  This layer is responsible for alerting the world about the messages of your subconcious and for attracting the needs programmed into your brain. Deep psychological, emotional, or otherwise challenging issues are observable in this layer. They will limit your ability to allow energies, the other two layers into your physical self. This layer can be contacted through the pineal gland, but also through the 12th auric field and chakra.

- **The second layer** of the energy egg looks like a thin line of energy that intersperses black energies and white energies. This layer attracts that which you imagine within your unconscious. You can call it the layer of wish making. If your programming is funky, you will assess energies that deter you from your destiny, or allow you to form fantasies that are unrealistic. If your use of the second layer is healthy, your twelfth chakra will enable the manifestation of desires into your life.

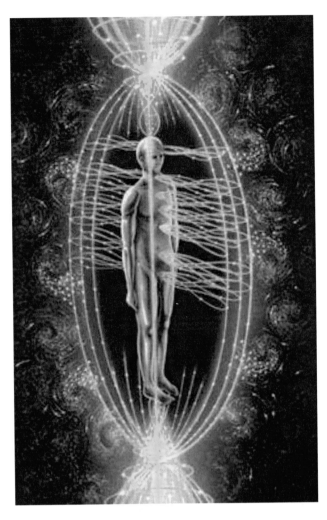

The third layer of the energy egg is a shimmering body of energy that interconnects the outer rim of the 12th chakra and auric field and the spiritual realms that lie beyond the human self. This layer attracts only that which fits your highest spiritual needs. It is therefore connected to your highest consciousness. It can actually call energies into your life that don't yet exist on this planet, to benefit you and others. The possibility for producing physical and emotional miracle lies in working this layer.

Cords, Contracts, Curses & Bindings

"Energetic lines - Energy Cords"

Inhibiting Contracts

All parts of the energetic anatomy (including chakras, auric fields, etc.) are susceptible to energetic challenges (including energetic contracts, and restrictions to accessing spiritual gifts and powers). These can and do affect every area of life, including physical health and relationship health. Psychically, this is what I look for:

Energetic cords: To me, they appear like thick tubing. The older and more limiting the contract, the thicker the tubing. Readable energy flows through the middle of these cords. When tapping in here, you can interpret the nature of the contract. For example, you know you have an energy cord if you feel it's impossible to disconnect from a person or group of people – no matter how hard you try. Orange energy, for instance, means exchange of feelings; yellow may indicate an exchange of beliefs; brown could indicate a generational issue.

    The image on the next page offers insight on what the energy cords may be imprinting and where.

    You (and/or your client) may have a multitude of cords from just one person. The reality is simple: most of us have cords, and they are from a variety of sources – including current partners, "ex's", friends, family, ancestors, and (yup!) entities.

    Lumin8 can be used as a supportive tool to petition the support we need to eliminate the cords.

    Cords are energetic connections between people, beings, or other aspects of self that serve as negative relationship contracts. Purpose and relationship are two sides of the same coin. (We need people to achieve our purpose, and purpose to clarify our relationships.)

Cords are formed when we contract with another person to meet our needs. This contract may seem beneficial on the surface, *until we realize that these contracts are usually formed out of fear and self-destructive beliefs.* These beliefs result in patterns that create self-destructive habits and limit the bonded relationships to a low standard of quality.

Cords are especially dangerous because they can be carried forth across time. **They may be formed soul-to-soul, mind-to-mind, or body-to-body during our existence (past lives or this life), or in any other soul/mind/body configuration.** They may directly or indirectly affect us but are almost always detrimental. (An exception is a cord between a mother and newborn, or in the case of a friend of mine, who offered her energy to save someone's life.) Cords generally gum up our energy system, filling holes that need to be there, clouding areas that need to be clear, and weakening barriers that need to be strong. In short, we cannot work efficiently—or at all—with our energy systems if we do not address our cords and the reasons we are holding them.

When Cords are Positive

• Cords can save someone's life
• Cords between a mother and a child, gradually reducing at these ages: 3 months; 6 months 1 year; 18 months & 3 years
• Temporary measure for teaching/transmission

Personal Exercise

- Think of someone you may have an unhealthy cord with.
- Determine what you are getting from the energy exchange. Ready to let it go?
- IMPORTANT: Determine how you can get your needs met in a way that honors your Spirit. (Most cords are an exchange of "You do this for me, I do that for you.") You will be more successful and will not succumb to reconnecting if you do this important step!
- Call in the support of the appropriate Lumin8 energies to support your healing. (I love the "Star Element" energy in conjunction with Angel Energy for this process.)

Example of Cording

Life energy cords look a lot like energetic cords with a distinction. The energy flowing through them is basic life energy. For this reason, they are psychically red or orange in color. These cords can exist between parts of the self, (such as in your current life to a past life self), or between a person and any other individual or group. Like wires running off a mainframe, they deliver electricity to the different end users, resulting in a "split" of your basic life energy, often into several "outlets". Energy depletion, chronic or severe illnesses, chronic fatigue, and adrenal problems usually involve life energy cords. One type of Life Energy Cord is your Vivaxis – which connects you to the place your mother spent the most time two weeks before you were born. Moving a cord like this one, is helpful when you have health challenges while, at the same time, that area becomes toxic due to environmental changes. Examples include: New cell phone towers installed, toxic waste deposit area, or added phone or electric lines. (Moving your vivaxis is something my Mastery Students have the opportunity to do whether they are healthy or not.)

Codependent contract/bargain. These are unique cords, usually originally formed between a parent and a child, that engender a two-way flow of energy. We give and we receive. Seems fine, right? However, in this case, the energy exchange always leaves the child lacking, because the cord establishes a bargain that creates a loss of the child's positive energy and an influx of a parent's undesirable energy. This energy exchange can be explained as a verbal contract between child and parent (respectively) – *even in adult years.* I had a friend who had this very contract with her mother. In essence the contract was this: She gave her life energy, took on her mother's pain and believed her mother kept her alive; her mother provided her spiritual gifts. Note: Incurring a codependent contract as a child allows the cord to form a bridge in our energetic boundaries and at least one chakra. This serves as a template for all other primary relationships, and becomes a healing opportunity the child has to deal with later in life.

Curses are thick, dark tubules bound together. They, too, can run between a person and any other individual or group. Curses are not empty at the center; the energy is bound in the tubes themselves. Curses hold diseases, sexual disorders, relationship issues and monetary challenges in place.

Bindings are like rubber bands that connect at least two beings and are often present in the first, fourth, fifth, ninth, and tenth chakras. A binding keeps the bound stuck together, usually lifetime after lifetime. Sometimes bindings are self-inflicted. Saying things like "I'll love you forever" creates a type of binding.

An energy marker looks like a clump of counter-clockwise swirling charges forming a symbol. This symbol will "instruct" others how to treat the marked. An energy marker in the tenth is usually mirrored in at least one other chakra and also patterned in the corresponding affected auric fields. Energy markers remind me of the "kick me" sign teens jokingly place on the back of a friend at school. Everyone responds to it – and you have no clue it's even there! If you're always treated disrespectfully, for instance, no matter your behavior, you might have an energy marker.

Holds are energy restrictions placed by one on another. A strong indicator of a hold is the feeling of being stuck. Often parents put holds on their children to keep them safe, but sometimes, unconsciously, they want to assure a steady diet of life energy.

Miasm is an energetic field that influences a group of souls or family members; often creates disease, beliefs, or thought patterns within family systems.

Healing with shape and Color

The easiest ways to address chakra imbalances and improve the correlating issue:
1. Uncover the beliefs and feelings holding an issue in place by accessing the wormholes of the future and the past (memory and imagination).
2. Address the spin, shape, colors, or symbols identified.

Strengthening your *visual psychic gifts* allows you to examine chakras for colors, discolorations and symbols. This can help you pinpoint an unhealthy chakra and therefore the root of the disease. You can then add and mix colors, symbols, and signs to encourage chakra healing. *Each psychic gift offers sight. I train my Mastery Students to "see" regardless of their natural predisposition.*

The 5 Universal Shapes featured in Lumin8 can be used to support healing and the chakric and energy body level, by simply placing the card over the designated chakra in the appropriate field.

Color & Chakra Healing

Below is a table that outlines healthy chakra colors.

Chakra	Color	Meaning
1	Red	Passion
2	Orange	Feelings and creativity
3	Yellow	Wisdom and power
4	Green	Healing
5	Blue	Communication and guidance
6	Purple	Vision
7	White	Spirituality

Here are a few suggestions to use on the primary path for checking colors:
The color of a chakra indicates the health of the individual and the current state of spiritual integration. A clear-colored chakra is (at least) fairly aligned with the Divine, enabling a connection with the spirit and increasing access to higher spiritual truths and powers. Discolorations, muddy, black tones, and/or off key colors indicate imbalance and disease. Very black or condensed areas can show entry points for energetic contracts or bindings, possessed energies, an influx of information-energy, or even aspects of someone else that doesn't belong within the system.

The Key: Consider the color that is off. Is it too slight, darkened, or off? What's the color? Link it to the chakra colors, for the most accurate shortcut in determining the chakra and auric fields in trouble.

The color and shape of a chakra reveal balance issues. If all the coloration is one-sided, you are missing half of the picture. Keep in mind that the strength and intensity of certain colors may be specific to a person's ethnic or cultural background. Correct the situation by shifting colors and energies until the color is balanced throughout the chakra.

The Meaning of Missing Colors

If you spot empty spaces where there ought to be color, shape, or form, some aspect of the self is fragmented and held in another aspect of self or elsewhere. "Elsewhere" can include another dimension, person or entity. Or it may indicate recession, sublimation of an aspect of the self. If recession is occurring, you will find an energy binding around empty space.

Color Your Healing

Using the following color charts, add colors to discolored or malformed chakras to create the necessary hues and configurations. Test the healing by reviewing the change the next day. If the coloration is off again, review the list of harmful colors. You can determine the possible rationale for chakra disturbance and then use other means to work out the issues. For instance, you might detect a black patch in the 1st chakra. You install the red energy of life, but the next day, discolorations have returned. Black represents issues of violation or evil. Now you can search for originating cause for this disturbance.

Spirit Enhancing Colors

Color	Meaning
Red	Life energy
Orange	Creativity and feelings
Yellow	Intellect
Pink	Love
Green	Healing
Blue	Communication
Purple	Vision, clarity & choices
White	Spirituality destiny

Harmful Colorations

Color	Meaning
Added Red Tones	Overstimulated passion, anger, ego or survival fears
Added Orange Tones	Emotionalism & hyperactivity
Added Yellow Tones	Overemphasizes ideas or beliefs to create judgments & delusions
Added Pink Tones	Can cause a sense of love where it doesn't exist
Added Green Tones	Overstimulates codependency and a need to "fix" what isn't broken
Added Blue Tones	Causes a need to over-explain
Added Purple Tones	Causes difficulty in planning, or making choices
Added White Tones	Overstimulates a need for religion, de-emphasizing action and power
Added Black Tones	Imbalances energies with emphasis on power, emotionalism, greed or powerlessness
Added Gold Tones	Causes excessive idealism and a resulting loss of hope
Added Silver Tones	Creates susceptibility to psychic sources
Added brown Tones	Causes confusion, mundane obsessions and/or excessive practicality
Added Grey Tones	Lack of clarity
Added Grey Tones	Lack of clarity

Healing with Shapes

There are 2 ways to accomplish simple diagnoses. The easiest is to examine the center of the chakra. Look to the middle of the chakra and ask to see which symbol is determining the current state of this repair. For example, you may see an X instead of a +, or misshapen or broken circles, squares or rectangles. Refer to the number and geometric symbol charts to determine the "causal symbols."

Then return to the Spirit-enhancing lists to figure out which symbols to substitute for the broken ones. Sometimes you do choose the equivalent symbol, such as a right-side-up 5-pointed star in place of an upside down one. Other times you need to provide a whole new symbol.

Geometric Shapes

The following is a generic list of meanings for major symbols, described in their healthy "spirit enhancing" states. You will see that the 5 Universal Shapes featured in Lumin8 are featured, among others.

Circle = Wholeness
Cross = Relationship; Human Divine Connection; Spiritual Connection
Square = Foundation
Triangle = Immortality/Vision/Preservation

Spiral = Growth; Cycles
Rectangle = Protection
5 Pointed Star = Alchemy; Movement
6 Pointed Star = Resurrection

Harmful Symbols
Altered Circle = Causes hurt, injury, damage, or separation
Altered Square = Used to overthrow or topple systems
Altered Rectangle = Imprisons or exposes to danger
Altered Triangle = Creates illness, disease, imbalance and death
Altered Spiral = Forces abrupt endings, cessation of cycles or rhythms
Altered 5 pointed star = Stifles, contains, and suffocates
Altered 6 pointed star = Causes "stuckness," despair and depression
Altered cross = Accentuates ego or causes extreme dejection
"X" Formation = Evil or anti-consciousness

More Chakra Healing Tips
By psychically seeing, repairing, and changing the chakra symbol or color, you can conduct a *Primary Healing* work. Here are a few tips:
- Find out if the current color or symbol is correct for the particular chakra. Compare with the symbols or colors in the ninth chakra. If it's correct, leave it alone.
- Examine the symbol for discoloration, irregular shape, or breaks. Incorrect or damaged symbols will cause chakra "disease" (and therefore life problems).
- Repair the symbol with intention, color, sound or other means, or add a new symbol to create a desired outcome.

3 Examples:

1. You can support a deeper **connection with your client and the Divine** by using 2 circles – 2 joined circles representing wholeness. If you want the relationship to assume its destined form, then color the circle white. If you want to direct healing, then color the circle green. If you desire harmony, use gold.

2. **Depression** is often indicated by a square holding muddy energy or an "off" symbol. The spiral, which represents growth, for example, may not be clean or may not be round, appearing to have jagged instead of smooth lines. Often, an aspect of the self is walled off. In cases like this, I use the Influential Path to clear the muddied areas and reveal the self. Then I infuse

the space with another color and corrected symbol, or use *"Heilstrom"* – (healing energy), ushered in by your client's Angels, Ancestors, Ascended Masters, Spirit Guides or the Creator (all featured in the Lumin8 Oracle) to be sure my client is getting the informed vibration I may not have determined. As with all symbols, you can analyze all aspects for diagnostic assistance. Consider the outside of the symbol, too, to determine the energies holding the emotion in place.

3. **Cancer** is complicated because there are so many components to it. In addition to the tumors themselves, there are the emotional and energetic components that need to be addressed. Personally, I accessed my guides to be sure the radiation treatment I was receiving only touched the areas that needed to be radiated. There was a relationship that was feeding the emotional component. I ended that relationship, and thus the emotional fuel that fed the cancer. Finally, I used symbols to support my healing process. (Each day I would use the Rune symbol Uruz, which helps you let go of the past, so you can receive your future. I simply traced the symbol over my heart – the chakra being compromised with cancer.)

Healing with Numbers

There are twelve numbers that are the most important for energetic healing. Below are the brief descriptions of their meanings when used appropriately and inappropriately. *The first 12 cards of the Lumin8 Oracle are Chakra cards that can double for numbers with intention.*

Spirit Enhancing Numbers:
1: Beginnings. Represents the Highest Form, the Creator.
2: Pairing and duality. Reflects that everything in the material universe is made of opposites—which are the same. A two splits unity, but also holds two ones in unity.
3: The number of creation. It lies between and emanates from a beginning and an ending.
4: Foundations and stability. The number of complete balance (consider a table, chair or home.)
5: Direction setting. Space for making decisions. Represents the human figure, able to go in every direction at once or travel at will.
6: Choices. The presence of light and dark, good and evil, and the gifts of love, as offered through free will.
7: Spiritual Principles. The Divine. The number of love and action that produces grace. Key number of the 3rd dimension.
8: Infinity. Recurring patterns and karma. Path of recycling. The number of knowledge.
9: Change. Elimination of what was. Can erase error and bring us to a new beginning.
10: New life. Release of the old and acceptance of the new. This number of physical matter can record the heavenly on earth.
11: Acceptance of what has been and what will be. Release of personal mythology. Opening to divine powers.
12: Mastery over human drama. Becoming ok with being fully human, and seeing the power in our humanity. Mastery of the human as divine.

Harmful Numbers (Altered Numbers)
Altered 1: Prevents us from reaching a conclusion.
Altered 2: Forces unhealthy liaisons and keeps victims stuck on the powerless side of power levels.
Altered 3: Causes chaos.
Altered 4: Imprisons or creates craziness.
Altered 5: Creates trickery or delusion.
Altered 6: The number of the lie. Causes confusion and disorder, convincing the victim to choose evil.
Altered 7: Establishes doubt about the Creator's very existence.
Altered 8: Stifles learning and forces the recycling of harmful patterns.
Altered 9: Instills terror and fear about change – keeping victims in the altered "8."

Altered 10: Prevents new beginnings and seeks to make victims continue the old ways.
Altered 11: Obliterates self-esteem and seeks to keep victims from accepting their humanity.
Altered 12: Disavows forgiveness and casts shadows over human goodness.

Geometric Symbol and Number Combinations

1- A dot or circle
2- Horizontal line
3- Triangle
4- Equal arm cross
5- Pentagram
6- Equilateral hexagram (Star of David or Merkabah)
7- Equilateral Septangle; a rainbow
8- Equilateral octagon
9- 3 Equilateral triangles
10- Circle with a cross of 8 arms or circle with square in the middle.
11- Parallel Lines
12- A rising sun with 12 lines; the lotus

Perform a Self-Scan. (If you are adventurous, draw an outline of a body – like a gingerbread man.) Grab colored pencils.

Preliminary How-To:

1. Notice your entire body from head to toe.

2. What is the primary color for your human self?

3. Are any areas dense with any particular colors?

4. Any immediate words, as phrases or stories that jump into your awareness? (Write these down.)

5. Any symbols? Document them.

6. Note whether there are energetic pulls or pushes – and where.

7. Focus on the compromised area. Ask it what it needs or wants.

8. If you're uncertain as to the origin you are evaluating, ask your body. Accept the first word, image or sensation that comes to mind.

Primary Energy Assessment Healing Techniques

When I was in science class (four score and one-hundred years ago), conversation about electrons, protons and neutrons made my eyes roll. If you are anything like me, know this: you don't have to be a scientist to get this. Simply pay attention to the ideas these notes represent, because I am going to bet you already (unknowingly) use this information.

There are several ways to access and direct basic energies for healing on the Primary Pathway. Here are a few:

Energy Particles and Charges

For health on the Primary Pathway, you must have balance between positive and negative charges in protons and electrons. Here are tips for determining where you lack balance.

Depleted Negative /Electrons (Overly positive/protons)	Depleted Positive/Protons (Overly negative/electrons)
Anxious, scared, can't settle down	Tired, depressed, lackluster
Managing energy bodies disconnected	Managing stuck energy bodies
Fear-based beliefs, feelings, & power levels	Shame-based beliefs, feelings
Chakras "wired," never spin in reverse	Chakras always spin in reverse
Auric field too thin	Auric field too thick
Coloration too light, won't hold "substance"	Coloration too dark or muddy/sticky
Chakric tones too high	Chakric tones too low
Issues future-based	Past the base shame/fear of what was
Overly psychic	Psychic sense too low

All Primary techniques are a way to balance the electro/proton energies in the body. Here are a few methods for using electrons, protons, neutrons and charges to actually accomplish healing.

Electron-Based Healing

Electrons are electric in nature. Sometimes their attachment to atoms is disconnected – actually miles away.

Electrons store what we consider negative feelings and beliefs, so a simple way to help someone (or yourself) is to work with the nature of electrons, using these three techniques:

Regressing to the Past: Electrons will congest in the place originating an issue. Let's say your issues with money started at a time in childhood, when you witnessed your parents fighting about bills. Or maybe you were not given what you wanted for your birthday because, you were told, your parents couldn't afford it.

Now – feel the issues of today. Concentrate on the negative effects listed on the previous page, then follow the energy and feelings listed to discover the electron base.

Recall the original trauma and self-defeating decisions. This information can be useful in understanding your issues or illness. Making a new decision can also transfer the change all the way into the present and reorganize the electrons you are currently working with.

Expanding the Present: Electrons follow logical pathways. If you are experiencing electrical-based issues, it's because you've taught your electrons to stay in a pattern. Breathe deeply and imagine that your current problem has transformed, healing has occurred.

Use your intuitive sight to watch the movement of the electrons that are holding this "new, healed state." Use intention to establish your chosen solution as true, at this "now" moment. Ask your Spirit what behaviors you need to adopt to permanently effect this change. (Reminder: there will be a physical component to it. *You will have to "do" something.*)

Owning the Future: There are many potential futures. In the psychic world, these time/spaces already exist. Select the one you want – that harmonizes with your spirit. What beliefs are you operating with in the future? What feelings keep you happy? Lock onto these fresh feelings and beliefs and download them into your wiring through intention. Ask your Spirit what behaviors you need to embrace to secure this resolution.

Proton-Based Healing

Protons encourage love and highlight our Spirit's dreams. Light particles within the protons can also move faster than the speed of light. Here are a few ways to work with proton healing:

Changing the past – Regression: What if your Spirit – the part of you always in connection with the Divine - managed your past? Think of how different your life would be if you saw past situations through the eyes of Love? Would you have made different choices?

Keep in mind that protons are attracted to neutrons or electrons and disappear when there is nothing to keep them in place. Look back at a difficult time, one that may have caused current issues. Where did the protons "live" before they gathered around the "causative situation"? What if they had never "lit up" the difficult event? If they had the opportunity to represent your Spirit, what would these protons choose to enlighten? Let your protons of your Spirit change what happened in the past. See what occurs.

Creating a New Present: Concentrate on a current problem – especially one causing you anxiety. Imagine that all the protons involved in the situation are centered inside of the issue. Now enlighten them. What spiritual **beliefs** underpin your current issue? What spiritual **idea** would alter the situation into a more positive one? Allow a switch of either protons or the information coded within them—and see what radiates forth.

Bringing Brightness to the Future: Ask to see the best potential outcome for a current state of affairs. The protons in this possible future will shine. See what you may need to do right now to create this reality. You can potentially transfer it into the here and now.

Neutron-Based Healing

Neutrons are neutral charges and hold the key to healing health issues. Here are several neutron-based healing techniques.

Get What's Going On: You may be thinking, "Why me? Why this?" The opportunity here is to move beyond the judgment for an elevated perspective. Ask the questions with the intention of getting the answers. Imagine you are standing on the neutron holding a situation in place and ask to psychically perceive the energetic reason for the situation.

Use Pink - The Color of Love: Neutrons can emit a pink charge that can heal electric issues. Think of your issue and ask what "anti-charge" you can intentionally release from your neutral self that will *love* a healing into place.

Use Gold Energy for Forceful Change: What if your situation requires more power? Gold energy demands forceful change...Are you willing to allow it?

Integration: Blending the magnetic and electrical aspects of yourself (or issue) is important. Have you ever witnessed anyone healed by the Holy Ghost? The healing involved in spiritual settings usually involves an opening of gold *magnetic* energy, which often heals spiritual issues and ideas about love.

But that calls into play the *electrical* side. It holds the wounds, pains and agonies – and splits from the magnetic spiritual side. Here, the wounded child is abandoned. With fundamentalist religious healings, the self has not healed. It has split.

The magnetic side becomes anxious, stretching towards the future, while the electrical side becomes depressed and stuck in the past. The issues are still present and projected toward others—who are then often perceived as "evil."

An equally dangerous route is to *overcome with the electric and deny the magnetic.* When we are overly material and also emotional, we tend to lean on money, sex, alcohol and other material resources – which then become our god. If our feelings are not transformed by spiritual energies, they remain body-based and their true meaning is difficult to discern. (Remember, what we resist, persists.)

Neutrons provide the ideal perspective for blending the better of the two sides. After healing an electrical or magnetic issue, "stand" in the place of the neutrons and link the two energies. In envisioning the healed state, you can picture dark matter (electrons) within the image and light around the image. Now, emanate pink and gold energy from the neutron to connect the different energies. Once the energies blend, the integration increases the healing effect.

Charges: Sometimes the information causing the situation departs, but the positive or negative energy charges do not leave. This is often seen in people who are cured then the illness returns, or lovers in an abusive relationship split – but the energy imprint of being "unlovable" or "unworthy" remains. A negative charge will be psychically dark and will cause electron-based issues. *Charges are held by elements.* Determine which element is holding the charge in place, and call in the contradicting element. For example, water puts out fire, while air can move or eliminate water.

Be sure to work toward bringing elements into the physical self through the primary means – such as diet and exercise and breath-work, in addition to the energy session.

The info below provides a "key" to Lumin8's 10 elements.

Remember that you yourself need to connect with each element, either in dream state or journey, to determine how each element is supportive.

1. **Fire:** Burns away, eliminates & purges. Adds life energy and excitement, often heralding the new. Can be used to purify the body (for example, lymph system, intestinal tract or blood) of toxins.
2. **Air:** Allows the spread of energies from person to person. Active when directed. Inactive (with amazing potential) when still. Can be used to destroy, or redirect. Perfect to use in "Spin Medicine."
3. **Water:** Transmits psychic and emotional energies. Soothes, heals, and cleanses. Between Intuitive sessions, imagine a pink waterfall of light that clears remaining energy. Water gazing, an intuitive technique, accesses the communicative power of water.
4. **Earth:** With earth, we hold walls and thought forms. We resume power to build, solidify and protect. Earth grounds and centers, and can be used to "rebuild" after surgery. Hold at the center of the first chakra. For those with manifesting issues (have too much Air) hold in the energy body fields.
5. **Metal:** Shields, protects, deflects and defends. Can be called in for cellular support, or placed around the auric field to deflect energies.
6. **Wood:** The perfect temporary measure for supporting adaptability. Useful in bringing joy to someone who is depressed, or increasing adaptability when we need to become acclimated to an unfamiliar environment.
7. **Stone:** Foundational energy. Strengthens, holds and supports. Perfect to use with the Water element (to hold it in place) in creating a healing reservoir. Or, use Stone with the first chakra and Fire Element to increase metabolism.
8. **Star:** Purification of physical matter through spiritual truth. Uses spiritual truth to form physical matter. Can be used to burn spiritual truth into any chakra to enable replenishment physically and psychically.
9. **Ether:** The Spiritual Energy. Science has attempted (for a millennia) to understand the Fifth Element. It holds Spiritual Truths and can be used to infuse any energy body.
10. **Light:** Electromagnetic radiation of various wavelengths. Light can be directed to produce any desired effect. Light-light is made mostly from protons that hold

information about love. Dark-light is made mostly from electrons that carry information about power.

When we're depressed, light-light can help us regain an enhanced perspective. If stuck, dark-light can help us move into action.

The Lumin8 Shamanic Journey Journal

Explore each Symbol in Lumin8 to uncover the opportunities and gifts that will support you and your clients.

Shamanism as a practice, includes reaching altered states of consciousness in order to perceive and interact with the spirit world and channel these transcendental energies into this world. It is an ancient healing tradition where you connect with nature and all of creation for healing, advice and teachings.

As all ancient spiritual practices are rooted in nature, shamanism is the method where we can strengthen that connection.

Shamanism stems from nature itself. Shamanic practices tap into the power of Mother Earth and the energies within and around her.

Shamanism is not only concerned with the health of the individual, but also with the health of the entire community. This includes all people, plants, animals and all of life. Daily spiritual practice allows for continued and exponential growth of both body and soul. The goal is to create internal and external harmony with all creation.

A Word on Journeying: Traditional Shamans detach from their bodies and travel to other dimensions to interact with otherworldly spirits. They do this through their soul, with imagination and intent. Shamans travel to the upper, middle and lower worlds, and often use drumming to facilitate the process.

I use my imagination and rhythmic breath to allow my soul to move across time and space. However you choose to journey, trust the information that you get. Write it down for future reference.

Chakra Cards: Journey to each of your chakras. See/Track what healing opportunities you discover.

Plant Spirits: Journey with each Plant Spirit. Let them share with you how they will support you and your clients.

Elements: Journey with each element to reveal a deeper meaning in the support they will offer.

Energy Bodies: Allow your Spirit to disengage from your body. Then explore each level of your being.

Emotions: Sit with each emotion card, and recall the times that emotion popped up for you. Feel, sense and imagine the emotion and where it may reside in your body.

Universal Shapes: Take the Preferential Shape Test. Have a full understanding of where you are now. Then do it for a friend!

Root Chakra

Sacral Chakra

Solar Plexus Chakra

Heart Chakra

Throat Chakra

3ʳᵈ Eye Chakra

Crown Chakra

8th Chakra

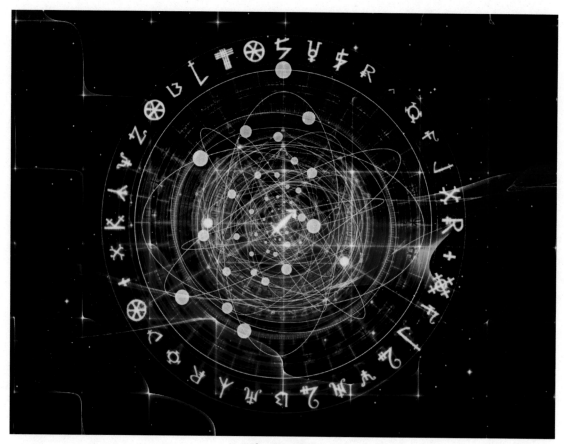

9th Chakra

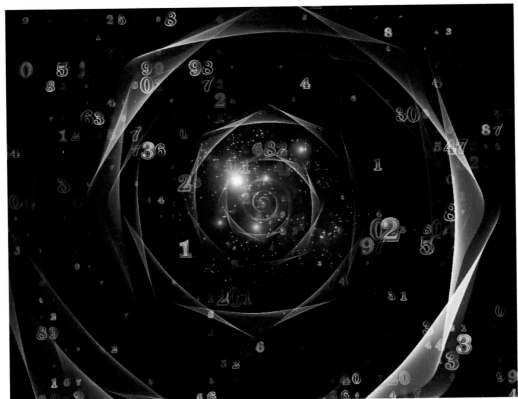

10th Chakra

11ᵗʰ Chakra

12th Chakra

Dandelion

When journeying to meet Dandelion, it appeared as a: Male   Female

What was most surprising was:_____

On my initial journey, Dandelion offered this:_____

_____

_____

_____

_____

On my second visit, Dandelion offered this: _____

_____

_____

_____

On my third visit, Dandelion offered this: _____

_____

_____

_____

_____

_____

Chamomile

When journeying to meet Chamomile, it appeared as a: Male   Female

What was most surprising was:_____.

On my initial journey, Chamomile offered this:_____
_____
_____
_____
_____

On my second visit, Chamomile offered this: _____
_____
_____
_____
_____

On my third visit, Chamomile offered this: _____
_____
_____
_____
_____
_____

Rose

When journeying to meet Rose, it appeared as a: Male   Female

What was most surprising was:_____.

On my initial journey, Rose offered this:_____

_____

_____

_____

On my second visit, Rose offered this: _____

_____

_____

_____

On my third visit, Rose offered this: _____

_____

_____

_____

_____

_____

Lavender

When journeying to meet Lavender, it appeared as a: Male   Female

What was most surprising was:_____.

On my initial journey, Lavender offered this:_____

_____

_____

_____

_____

On my second visit, Lavender offered this: _____

_____

_____

_____

_____

On my third visit, Lavender offered this: _____

_____

_____

_____

_____

_____

Mugwort

When journeying to meet Mugwort it appeared as a: Male   Female

What was most surprising was:_____.

On my initial journey, Mugwort offered this:_____

_____

_____

_____

On my second visit, Mugwort offered this: _____

_____

_____

_____

On my third visit, Mugwort offered this: _____

_____

_____

_____

_____

_____

Holy Basil

When journeying to meet Holy Basil, it appeared as a: Male   Female

What was most surprising was:_____

On my initial journey, Holy Basil offered this:_____

_____

_____

_____

_____

On my second visit, Holy Basil offered this: _____

_____

_____

_____

_____

On my third visit, Holy Basil offered this: _____

_____

_____

_____

_____

_____

Nettle

When journeying to meet Nettle, it appeared as a: Male   Female

What was most surprising was:_____.

On my initial journey, Nettle offered this:_____

_____

_____

_____

_____

On my second visit, Nettle offered this: _____

_____

_____

_____

_____

On my third visit, Nettle offered this: _____

_____

_____

_____

_____

_____

Calendula

When journeying to meet Calendula, it appeared as a: Male   Female

What was most surprising was:_____

On my initial journey, Calendula offered this:_____

_____

_____

_____

_____

On my second visit, Calendula offered this: _____

_____

_____

_____

_____

On my third visit, Calendula offered this: _____

_____

_____

_____

_____

_____

_____

Echinacea

When journeying to meet Echinacea, it appeared as a: Male   Female

What was most surprising was:_____

On my initial journey, Echinacea offered this:_____

_____

_____

_____

On my second visit, Echinacea offered this: _____

_____

_____

_____

On my third visit, Echinacea offered this: _____

_____

_____

_____

_____

_____

Star of Bethlehem

When journeying to meet Star of Bethlehem, it appeared as a: Male   Female

What was most surprising was:_____

On my initial journey, Star of Bethlehem offered this:_____

_____

_____

_____

_____

On my second visit, Star of Bethlehem offered this: _____

_____

_____

_____

On my third visit, Star of Bethlehem offered this: _____

_____

_____

_____

_____

_____

Sage

When journeying to meet Sage, it appeared as a: Male   Female
What was most surprising was:_____.
On my initial journey, Sage offered this:_____
_____
_____
_____
_____

On my second visit, Sage offered this: _____
_____
_____
_____

On my third visit, Sage offered this: _____
_____
_____
_____
_____
_____

Rosemary

When journeying to meet Rosemary, it appeared as a: Male   Female

What was most surprising was:_____

On my initial journey, Rosemary offered this:_____
_____
_____
_____
_____

On my second visit, Rosemary offered this: _____
_____
_____
_____

On my third visit, Rosemary offered this: _____
_____
_____
_____
_____
_____

Earth

When journeying to meet Earth, it appeared as: Male   Female   Other_____

What was most surprising was:_____

On my initial journey, Earth offered this:_____

_____

_____

_____

_____

On my second visit, Earth offered this: _____

_____

_____

_____

_____

On my third visit, Earth offered this: _____

_____

_____

_____

_____

_____

Air

When journeying to meet Air, it appeared as: Male   Female   Other:_____

What was most surprising was:_____

On my initial journey, Air offered this:_____

_____

_____

_____

_____

On my second visit, Air offered this: _____

_____

_____

_____

On my third visit, Air offered this: _____

_____

_____

_____

_____

_____

Water

When journeying to meet Water, it appeared as: Male   Female   Other_____

What was most surprising was:_____.

On my initial journey, Water offered this:_____

_____

_____

_____

_____

On my second visit, Water offered this: _____

_____

_____

_____

_____

On my third visit, Water offered this: _____

_____

_____

_____

_____

_____

_____

Fire

When journeying to meet Fire, it appeared as: Male   Female   Other_____

What was most surprising was:_____

On my initial journey, Fire offered this:_____

_____

_____

_____

_____

On my second visit, Fire offered this: _____

_____

_____

_____

_____

On my third visit, Fire offered this: _____

_____

_____

_____

_____

_____

Star

When journeying to meet Dandelion, it appeared as: Male   Female Other_____

What was most surprising was:_____.

On my initial journey, Dandelion offered this:_____

_____

_____

_____

On my second visit, Dandelion offered this: _____

_____

_____

_____

On my third visit, Dandelion offered this: _____

_____

_____

_____

_____

_____

Light

When journeying to meet Light, it appeared as: Male   Female   Other_____

What was most surprising was:_____.

On my initial journey, Light offered this:_____

_____

_____

_____

_____

On my second visit, Light offered this: _____

_____

_____

_____

On my third visit, Light offered this: _____

_____

_____

_____

_____

_____

Wood

When journeying to meet Wood, it appeared as: Male   Female   Other_____
What was most surprising was:_____.
On my initial journey, Wood offered this:_____
_____
_____
_____

On my second visit, Wood offered this: _____
_____
_____
_____

On my third visit, Wood offered this: _____
_____
_____
_____
_____
_____

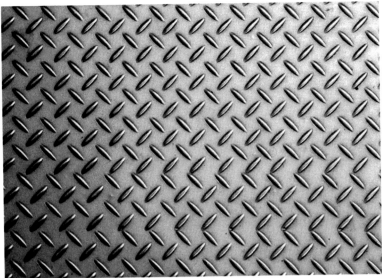

Metal

When journeying to meet Metal, it appeared as: Male   Female   Other_____

What was most surprising was:_____.

On my initial journey, Metal offered this:_____

_____

_____

_____

On my second visit, Metal offered this: _____

_____

_____

_____

On my third visit, Metal offered this: _____

_____

_____

_____

_____

Stone

When journeying to meet Stone, it appeared as: Male   Female   Other_____

What was most surprising was:_____

On my initial journey, Stone offered this:_____

_____

_____

_____

_____

_____

On my second visit, Stone offered this: _____

_____

_____

_____

_____

On my third visit, Stone offered this: _____

_____

_____

_____

_____

_____

_____

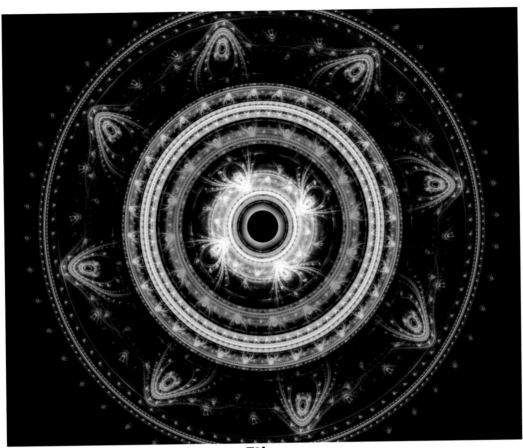

Ether

When journeying to meet Ether, it appeared as a: Male   Female   Other

What was most surprising was:_____.

On my initial journey, Ether offered this:_____
_____
_____
_____
_____

On my second visit, Ether offered this: _____
_____
_____
_____

On my third visit, Ether offered this: _____
_____
_____
_____
_____

Angels

When journeying to meet my Angel, it appeared as a: Male   Female   Other_____

What was most surprising was:_____.

On my initial journey, my Angel offered this:_____

_____

_____

_____

_____

On my second visit, my Angel offered this: _____

_____

_____

_____

On my third visit, my Angel offered this: _____

_____

_____

_____

_____

_____

Ascended Masters

When journeying to meet my Ascended Master, it/they appeared as: Male   Female
What was most surprising was:_____.
On my initial journey, my Ascended Master offered this:_____
_____
_____
_____
_____

On my second visit, my Ascended Master offered this: _____
_____
_____
_____
_____

On my third visit, my Ascended Master offered this: _____
_____
_____
_____
_____
_____

Ancestors

When journeying to meet my Ancestors, I met: _____

What was most surprising was:_____

On my initial journey, my Ancestor offered this:_____

_____

_____

_____

_____

On my second visit, my Ancestor offered this: _____

_____

_____

_____

On my third visit, my Ancestor offered this: _____

_____

_____

_____

_____

_____

Spirit Guides

When journeying to meet my Spirit Guide, it appeared as a: Male   Female

What was most surprising was:_____.

On my initial journey, Spirit Guide offered this:_____
_____
_____
_____
_____

On my second visit, Spirit Guide offered this: _____
_____
_____
_____
_____

On my third visit, Spirit Guide offered this: _____
_____
_____
_____
_____
_____

Star Beings

When journeying to meet Star Being, it appeared as a: Male   Female

What was most surprising was:_____.

On my initial journey, Star Being offered this:_____

_____

_____

_____

On my second visit, Star Being offered this: _____

_____

_____

_____

On my third visit, Star Being offered this: _____

_____

_____

_____

_____

_____

Creator

When journeying to meet the Creator, it appeared as a: Male   Female

What was most surprising was:_____

On my initial journey, Creator offered this:_____

_____

_____

_____

_____

_____

On my second visit, Creator offered this: _____

_____

_____

_____

_____

On my third visit, Creator offered this: _____

_____

_____

_____

_____

_____

_____

Joy

When I connect to the emotion of Joy, I feel it mostly in my:_____.
The images I see in my mind's eye are:

_____
_____

The memories I have include:

_____
_____
_____

My other senses include:

_____
_____
_____
_____
_____

Anger

When I connect to the emotion of Anger, I feel it mostly in my:_____.
The images I see in my mind's eye are:
_____
_____
_____

The memories I have include:
_____
_____
_____
_____

My other senses include:
_____
_____
_____
_____
_____

Fear

When I connect to the emotion of Fear, I feel it mostly in my:_____.
The images I see in my mind's eye are:
_____
_____
_____

The memories I have include:
_____
_____
_____
_____

My other senses include:
_____
_____
_____
_____
_____

Sadness

When I connect to the emotion of Sadness, I feel it mostly in my:_____.
The images I see in my mind's eye are:

_____

_____

_____

The memories I have include:

_____

_____

_____

_____

My other senses include:

_____

_____

_____

_____

_____

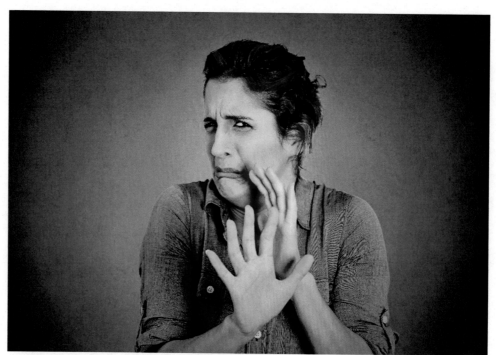

Disgust

When I connect to the emotion of Disgust, I feel it mostly in my:_____.

The images I see in my mind's eye are:

_____
_____
_____

The memories I have include:

_____
_____
_____
_____

My other senses include:

_____
_____
_____
_____
_____

Physical Body

Emotional Body

Mental Body

Spiritual Body

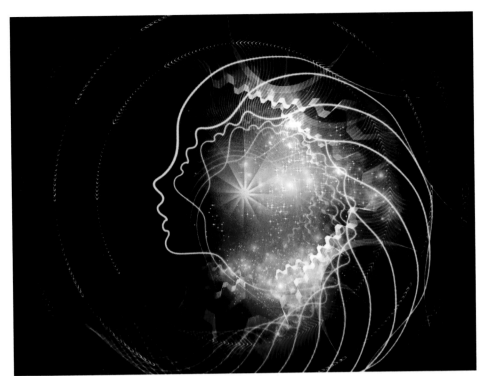

Soul

Case Studies

Your Lumin8 Case Studies:
The best way to honor the gifts inherent in you is through validation and confirmation. The following pages allow you to journal your experiences with the Elements, Plant Spirits, Shapes, Chakras, Energy Bodies and clients to gain the insight that will support your practice.

CASE STUDIES: This is where you become more comfortable working with others through experience. Give yourself permission to use the following as a guide, so you can document results and lessons learned.

Client Name:_____

Client Concern: _____

Primary Site/Energy Center: _____

Energy Body: _____

Comments:
_____
_____
_____
_____
_____
_____
_____

Remedy 1._____

Remedy 2._____

Remedy 3. _____

Homework:_____
_____
_____

Client Name:_____

Client Concern: _____

Primary Site/Energy Center: _____

Energy Body: _____

Comments:

_____
_____
_____
_____
_____
_____
_____

**Remedy
1.**_____

**Remedy
2.**_____

Remedy 3. _____

Homework:_____
_____
_____
_____
_____
_____

Client Name:_____

Client Concern: _____

Primary Site/Energy Center: _____

Energy Body: _____

Comments:

_____
_____
_____
_____
_____
_____
_____
_____

Remedy
1._____

Remedy
2._____

Remedy 3. _____

Homework:_____

_____
_____
_____
_____
_____

Client Name:_____

Client Concern: _____

Primary Site/Energy Center: _____

Energy Body: _____

Comments:

_____
_____
_____
_____
_____
_____
_____

Remedy
1._____

Remedy
2._____

Remedy 3. _____

Homework:_____
_____
_____
_____
_____
_____

Client Name: _____

Client Concern: _____

Primary Site/Energy Center: _____

Energy Body: _____

Comments:

_____
_____
_____
_____
_____
_____
_____
_____

Remedy
1. _____

Remedy
2. _____

Remedy 3. _____

Homework: _____

_____
_____
_____
_____
_____

Client Name:_____

Client Concern: _____

Primary Site/Energy Center: _____

Energy Body: _____

Comments:

_____
_____
_____
_____
_____
_____
_____

Remedy
1._____

Remedy
2._____

Remedy 3. _____

Homework:_____

_____
_____
_____
_____
_____

Client Name:_____

Client Concern: _____

Primary Site/Energy Center: _____

Energy Body: _____

Comments:

_____
_____
_____
_____
_____
_____
_____

Remedy
1._____

Remedy
2._____

Remedy 3. _____

Homework:_____

_____
_____
_____
_____
_____

I hope you have enjoyed your journey with
The Lumin8 Healing Oracle!

If you have taken the time to go through at least half of the exercises and embraced the material, you are a *Lumin8-er*... helping yourself through a heightened level of awareness that benefits you and those around you.

Want to take your intuitive powers to the next level? Consider taking the **Lumin8 On-line program. (visit GinaSpriggs.Guru)**
    This program is designed to support your personal power and growth in the most authentic way possible. Many of those who enroll in my programs go on to become professional Intuitives in service of others - either supplementing their income or stepping into this arena full time.
    It is my honor sharing the wisdom I have gained over years of experience, training and from teachers from around the world.

You Are Loved ~

Gina Spriggs

Suggested Reading/Resources:
The Subtle Body Practice Manual, Cyndi Dale
The Subtle Body, Cyndi Dale
Shaman, Healer, Sage, Alberto Villoldo
The Intuitive Tarot Workbook, Gina Spriggs
The Hearts Code, Paul P. Pearsall